TIMBERS OF THE WORLD...

5

PHILIPPINES and JAPAN

Prepared by **W. H. Brown**, FIWSc
In collaboration with TRADA publications panel

Published by
TIMBER RESEARCH AND DEVELOPMENT ASSOCIATION
Hughenden Valley, High Wycombe, Buckinghamshire HP14 4ND, England

AVAILABILITY
Before specifying, it is advisable to check on the commercial
availability of the timbers described in this booklet.

PRINTING HISTORY
First published 1978

ISBN 0 901348 47 3

Typography by Trevor Tredwell, AMIM Ptg
Maps prepared by Tim Wheeler, Henley-on-Thames
Printed by Executive Press Ltd, Burnham, Bucks

CONTENTS

Introduction

Timbers of Philippines and Japan

PART I HARDWOODS

PART II SOFTWOODS

INTRODUCTION

The geographical scope of this booklet is confined to that part of Asia that includes the islands of Japan and the extensive Philippine Islands.

Japan

Japan consists of a long, narrow, and continuous chain of volcanic islands in the north west of the Pacific Ocean. Its northern limit is the coast of Hokkaido, south of the Kuril Islands, and its southern extreme at Tokuno Island, north of Okinawa. The islands are bounded on the west by the Korea Strait and the Sea of Japan, and on the east by the Pacific.

The principal islands forming Japan are Honshu, the mainland or main country; Kyushu; Shikoku; Oki Gunto; Osumi Gunto; Tsushima, in the Korea Strait; Awaji, lying between Shikoku and the main island, sacred in the eyes of all Japanese as the first spot on earth to be evolved out of chaos by the gods of heaven at the creation of the world, and to the north, beyond Honshu, Hokkaido, one of the largest islands of the whole archipelago.

Honshu is the largest, wealthiest, and most populous of the islands with an area of some 233 000 square kilometres, while Hokkaido, separated from Honshu by the narrow Tsugaru Straits, has an area a little less than that of Ireland as a whole.

Climate

Japan is subject to greater extremes of heat and cold than England, climatic conditions largely contributing to the comparatively slow growth of trees and the resulting mildness of much of their timber, for example oak and beech.

Hokkaido is usually buried in deep snow during the long winter of four or five months, and the same may be said of all the provinces of the west coast of the main island, which are further exposed to the bitter winds from the Sea of Japan. The east coast is comparatively mild, due to the influence of the Kuro Siwo or Black Stream, the 'Gulf Stream' of the Pacific, which, flowing north from the tropical seas south of the Philippines, strikes the coast of Kyushu in the south-east, and its main flow then skirts the whole of the east coast until finally it is lost in the waters of the northern Pacific. It brings with it warmth and moisture from the tropics and exercises an influence similar to that of the Gulf Stream on the shores of Britain.

In the southern islands the climate and the vegetation are both sub-tropical, and apart from mountain tops, snow is unknown. On average, the mean annual temperature in Tokyo is 14°C (57°F), the mean maximum is 30°C (86°F), and the mean minimum, minus 2°C (28°F). The highest temperature recorded on any one day is 36.5°C (98°F) in July, and the lowest, minus 9°C (15°F) in January.

The average rainfall is 3680mm and the average number of days on which either rain or snow fall is 140. The wettest months are June and September, the recognised two rainy seasons, during which torrential rain is often continuous without a break for several days. The first three months of the year are cold and damp, but April and May are generally delightful and seldom marred by high winds or heavy showers, but by far the pleasantest season is the Autumn from October to December, a period known as the Koharu, or Little Spring, when fine weather, with bracing air and blue skies can be relied upon.

In few countries are tropical and temperate vegetation so mingled as in Japan, where trees of Europe and North America, such as elm, beech, oak and chestnut grow almost side by side with bamboo, sugar cane, and tobacco of tropical Asia.

Commercial centres

The increase of manufactured goods since 1945 has produced a steady increase in the urban population, the tendency to migrate to the towns and cities being more marked than anywhere else in the world, and essential to sustain the vast industrial enterprises in the island of Honshu particularly. The great ports and harbours of Osaka, Tokyo, Kobe and Yokohama being principal areas for foreign trade, but as with America and the UK imports of timber form an essential ingredient of industry, and Japan today imports considerable amounts of timber, especially from the Philippines.

Philippine Islands

The Philippines are an extensive group of islands, more than 3000 in number, and with the Sulu Islands cover a land surface of about 300 000 square kilometres. The principal islands are Luzon, Mindanao, Paragua, Negros, Panay, Samar, Mindoro, Bohol, Cebu, Leyte, and Masbate. Manila is the capital.

The northern extremity of the group is at Batan, South-east of Taiwan, the southernmost point is Jolo in the Celebes Sea, and the islands are bounded on the east by the Pacific, and on the west by the South China Sea.

Mainly of volcanic origin, the Philippines are traversed by irregular mountain ranges, well clothed in vegetation and separated by plains of great fertility, watered by innumerable lakes and rivers, affording ample means of transport.

The climate is tropical; rain from the south-west monsoon falls between June and September on the west coasts, and from October the north-east trade winds bring rain to the east coasts. The mean annual temperature throughout the islands is 27°C (80°F).

The indigenous flora is generally similar to the Malaysian, with the addition of some more northern varieties, and also a few Australian genera.

Although large forest areas still exist throughout the islands, much timber was destroyed in the fighting in the last war, and recovery is not only a slow process, but since considerable efforts are being made to increase the food supply of the Philippines, land clearance schemes have reduced to a degree some previously well-forested areas. Exports of timber to a great extent are confined to the Dipterocarps, especially the lauans; other types are more generally absorbed in home consumption, often on an inter-island basis.

Durability

Durability, or resistance to decay is important when woods are selected for certain uses where the conditions are favourable for decay to develop. Sapwood is nearly always perishable, but generally more permeable than heartwood, consequently it should not be used in exposed situations without preservative treatment. Heartwood varies in its natural resistance to decay according to the species and the degree of decay inhibiting substances contained in the wood.

The various grades of durability mentioned in the text are those resulting from exposure tests carried out in the United Kingdom, and accordingly are approximate values applicable to areas with similar climate.

The tests refer to all-heartwood stakes of 50mm x 50mm section driven in the ground. The five durability grades are defined as follows.

Perishable	Less than 5 years when in contact with the ground.
Non-durable	5-10 years when in contact with the ground.
Moderately durable	10-15 years when in contact with the ground
Durable	15-25 years when in contact with the ground.
Very durable	More than 25 years when in contact with the ground

Layout

The timbers described in this booklet are in two parts, ie hardwoods and softwoods, and wherever possible, commercial names follow closely the classification given in BS 881 and 589; 'Nomenclature of commercial timbers, including sources of supply'; 1974.

The text is supplemented by a Use Guide, given at the end of the booklet, together with notes on the relative resistance of heartwood to preservative treatment and to termite attack.

A list of companion booklets in this series of World Timbers is also given, and it is hoped that the comprehensive coverage provided will inspire a wider appreciation of the world's timber resources and make easier the inevitable acceptance of lesser-known species which progressively are appearing on the world's timber markets.

PART I HARDWOODS

AGARU

Dysoxylum decandrum Merr.   Family : Meliaceae

Other names
paluahan, bagulibas, buntugon.

Distribution
Various species of *Dysoxylum* occur in tropical Asia and Australia, and a number are also found in the Philippines, although fairly scattered throughout their distribution.

General characteristics
D. decandrum is a medium-size tree, with a straight bole, and a diameter of about 0.6m.

The sapwood is light yellow in colour, 20mm to 30mm wide, and rather sharply, but irregularly marked off from the heartwood which is light yellow when freshly cut, turning to light yellowish-brown during drying, the colour shading gradually from the lighter inner edge to the darker outer edge of each growth ring. The grain is commonly wavy, giving a beautiful moiré silk effect to the wood. The texture is fine, dense, and smooth and, when fresh, the wood has a characteristic odour reminiscent of sandalwood ; this disappears superficially on drying, but is restored if the wood is scraped or cut.

The timber is easy to dry without excessive degrade, easy to work and machine, and is classified as durable, when used in contact with the ground. Weight about 721 kg/m^3 when dried.

Uses
Agaru is similar in general appearance and mechanical properties to Indian satinwood (*Chloroxylon swietenia*), and therefore suitable for high-class furniture and cabinet-work, and to some extent is used in the Philippines for these purposes, but due to its scattered growth, it does not appear in regular quantities on the Manila market, and appears to find a more limited local use in building construction for posts, beams, joists and rafters, flooring, windows and sills, doors and as hewn railway ties.

AGOHO

Casuarina equisetifolia Forst.   Family : Casuarinaceae

Distribution
Occurs in the Philippines in almost pure stands on sandy shores, extending inland along streams and in sandy river beds of 800m elevation.

The tree
A small tree, it may reach a height of 50m but is usually smaller, with a diameter of 0.9m and a clear bole length of about 10m.

The timber
The sapwood is wide and buff-coloured but distinct from the heartwood which is light-red or dark reddish-brown, often with darker, narrow lines of parenchyma. The grain is straight, occasionally crossed, with a fine to moderately fine texture, while the wood is heavy to extremely heavy, weighing on average 1060 kg/m³ when dried.

Drying
Difficult to dry and prone to check and warp even under ordinary air drying. Partial air drying under cover is recommended prior to kiln drying.

Strength
The strength of agoho closely approximates to that of selangan batu merah (*Shorea guiso*) of Sabah.

Durability
Moderately durable.

Working qualities
Rather difficult to work, the wood adjacent to the large rays tending to crumble and tear in sawing and planing, but bearing in mind the uses for the timber, finishing quality may not be important.

Uses
Beams, joists, and foundation piling in buildings and house construction. Also for tool handles.

AILANTHUS

Ailanthus altissima Swingle   Family: Simarubaceae
syn. *A. glandulosa* Desf.

Other names
tree of heaven.

Distribution
Found in eastern Asia, northern Australia, and indigenous in China, in the northern provinces, and occurs in Japan.

General characteristics
A tall, straight tree, some 30m in height, with a diameter of 1.0m whose pinnate leaves give it a superficial appearance of ash (*Fraxinus* spp.) when seen growing in the UK where it was introduced, but in China and Japan, the leaves are longer, spreading palm-like from the ends of branches.
The timber is similar to ash in general appearance, and may be mistaken for it at first glance, but ailanthus is usually more white in colour, as opposed to the yellowish or brownish cast more typical of ash. Close examination of end grain however serves to distinguish the species since ash has its late-wood pores generally in pairs, while those in ailanthus are in clusters arranged tangentially, while the rays are larger in ailanthus. Both woods are ring porous.
Ailanthus is an elastic wood with a fine satiny sheen, but is of minor commercial importance, although used locally for joinery and for cabinets.

ALBIZIA SPECIES

Albizia spp.   Family: Leguminosae

Various species of the genus *Albizia* occur in the Philippines, all having a wide, whitish-coloured sapwood, and light to dark brown, durable heartwood, the colour varying with the species and growth conditions.

Albizia acle Merr. produces acle, otherwise known as akli. Acle is probably the most important species; a hard, moderately heavy to heavy timber, weighing from 608 kg/m³ to 660 kg/m³ when dried. The whitish sapwood is up to 50mm wide, sharply defined from the heartwood which is pale, dull brown to dark walnut-brown. The colouring matter is soluble in water and alcohol, and the wood has a strong peppery odour, the dust often causing unpleasant sneezing when worked, especially when very dry wood is machined.

The bole of the tree is often crooked, and this gives rise to grain which is sometimes very curly or crossed, and the texture is rather coarse but even.

Uses

General construction, sills, posts, sleepers, and from selected logs, furniture, cabinets and high-class interior joinery. The wood is very durable.

A. marginata Merr. produces a timber known as unik. This is a soft, light-weight wood, about 512 kg/m³ when dried, with a whitish sapwood gradually merging into the pale, pinkish-brown or reddish-brown heartwood, often with conspicuous broad growth rings. The grain is almost perfectly straight, and the texture fairly fine. The timber is moderately durable.

Uses

Since its distribution appears confined to Luzon, its commercial value is limited, but it is used locally for bancas (long seats or benches typical of the Philippines), interior trim and ceilings, and for cases for shipping cigarettes.

A. procera Benth. produces a timber known as acleng-parang. This is a hard, moderately heavy to heavy timber, weighing about 848 kg/m³ when dried, with a rich, dark chestnut-brown heartwood, generally with conspicuous irregular darker and lighter bands, with a straight grain, and fine, glossy texture. Said to be durable.

Uses

Acleng-parang is sometimes sold as an alternative to acle, and is used for similar purposes, but it has a rather wider use and this includes carving, gun stocks and agricultural implements.

4

A. retusa Benth. produces kasai, a timber very similar in appearance to acleng-parang, but a little lighter in colour, used for general construction and interior joinery.

A. saponaria Bl. produces salingkugi, very similar to kasai.

A. lebbeck Benth. which produces kokko of India and Burma, also occurs in the Philippines, and is cultivated in some of the islands, particularly in Luzon. This is a dark, walnut-brown wood, with darker markings, weighing about 650 kg/m³ when dried, moderately durable, and used for general construction, furniture, and sliced for decorative veneer.

A. lebbekoiodes Benth. produces kariskis, a timber very similar to acleng-parang.

ALDER, JAPANESE

Alnus glutinosa Gaertn.   Family: Betulaceae

Other names
The Japanese name for alder is hannoki, and this should not be confused with hinoki (cypress), or honoki (magnolia).

Distribution
Widely distributed from Europe, North Africa, into Asia, and Japan.

The tree
Generally reaches a height of 15m to 27m and a diameter of about 0.5m when the conditions are favourable, but often with a clear bole of no more than 6m or 7m and a diameter of 0.3m.

The timber
There is no general difference in colour between sapwood and heartwood, the wood being a pale reddish-brown colour, and rather more red than the same species found in Europe. It is a dull, featureless wood, except for some darker-coloured lines or streaks appearing on longitudinal surfaces, due to the broad rays.
The timber weighs about 530 kg/m³ when dried.

Drying
The timber dries fairly rapidly and without undue degrade.

Strength
A soft, weak timber, similar to poplar in general strength.

Durability
A relatively easy timber to convert and machine, although sharp, thin-edged cutters are required in order to ensure a regular smooth finish in planing and moulding. The wood turns reasonably well, and can be stained, polished, glued and nailed without difficulty.

Uses
Turnery, usually in the form of rollers, broom handles, brush parts, clog soles and for plywood. Gnarled pieces are frequently used in Japan as decorative media.

AMUGIS

Koordersiodendron pinnatum Merr.　　Family : Anacardiaceae

Other names
ambugis, mugis, amugis perfecto. (See also *Palaquium* spp.)

Distribution
A tall, straight tree, up to 1.0m in diameter, widely, but sparsely distributed throughout the Philippines.

General characteristics
The sapwood is up to 50mm wide, pale, dull red in colour, rather sharply defined from the heartwood which is a dull, coppery red. The grain is usually straight, but sometimes with short, regular waves, and often with numerous, very small knots. The wood is moderately hard to hard, and fairly heavy, weighing 800 kg/m³ to 881 kg/m³ when dried.

Uses
The timber is moderately durable and is used for beams, joists and rafters, and for vehicle bodies, flooring, furniture and cabinets.

Note: several other reddish coloured woods are often loosely called amugis as follows,

Bassia ramiflora Merr. or baniti or amugis. Sapotaceae family.

Buchaniana arborescens Bl. or balinghasay or amugis. Anacardiaceae family.

Garuga spp. or bogo or amugis. Burseraceae family.

APITONG

Dipterocarpus spp.   Family: Dipterocarpaceae

Other names
bagac, Philippine gurjun.

Distribution
Widely distributed throughout the Philippines, especially in regions where the dry season is pronounced.

The tree
A lightly buttressed tree reaching a height of 30m to 40m and a diameter of 1.8m with a straight, cylindrical bole of about 25m to 30m.

The timber
The sapwood is 40mm to 60mm wide, pale brown in colour, and not sharply defined from the heartwood which is reddish to light brown. The grain is occasionally wavy and slightly crossed, and the texture, variable in different regions, ranges from moderately fine to moderately coarse. The wood contains a sticky resin which sometimes exudes on the surface of sawn material.
Three species principally supply apitong, ie *Dipterocarpus gracilis* Bl., *D. grandiflorus* Blanco. and *D. lasiopodus* Perkins,

and the weight of the wood varies according to species and to growth conditions, but an average is about 740 kg/m³ when dried.

Drying
Apitong is difficult to dry because it checks and warps even in ordinary air drying under Philippine air conditions, and it is susceptible to collapse when kiln dried from the green. Slow, partial air drying prior to kiln drying is recommended, and in experimental drying tests it was found that pre-steaming the green timber from the saw at 212°F in saturated condition for about two hours before the air drying and kiln drying processes, facilitated drying and minimized excessive degrade.

Strength
Compared with teak, air dry apitong is about 25 per cent stiffer, and 40 per cent more resistant to shock loads ; in other strength categories, apitong is about equal to teak.

Durability
Moderately durable.

Working qualities
The timber is variable in its working properties. Resin may be troublesome in some cases, and negligible in others, while cutter wear may be rapid at times and less so in other parcels. In general, apitong planes and moulds to a clean, slightly fibrous finish, but there is an inclination for the grain to pick up in quarter-sawn material unless a cutting angle of not more than 20° is used. It takes nails and screws well, and can be stained without difficulty but the presence of resin may call for care in varnishing and polishing.
Cold logs of apitong are fairly easy to peel on the veneer lathe, but pre-heating logs in hot water promotes exudation of resin, thereby improving peeling quality.

Uses
The standard wood for all types of piling in the Philippines, it is also commonly used for building construction, posts, framing and flooring. Creosoted apitong is the premier wood for transmission poles and railway ties.

ARANGA

Homalium spp.   Family: Flacourtiaceae

About ten species of *Homalium* occur in the Philippines, most of them producing commercial timber, the largest trees having a diameter of about 1.0m.
The most important species are as follows,
H. luzoniense F.-Vill. produces typical aranga, or arangan.
H. bracteatum Benth. produces arangan.
H. oblongifolium Merr. produces aranga.
H. villarianum Vid. produces adanga, or matobato.

General characteristics
The general appearance, mechanical properties, and structure of these various species are very much alike except for slight variations in colour and density, which appear to be related more to local growth conditions rather than to species differences.
The wood of all species is hard and heavy, varying from 864 kg/m³ to 881 kg/m³ when dried. The sapwood, up to 50mm wide, is yellowish or pinkish, in some species sharply defined, in others merging gradually into the heartwood, which is very variable, ranging from yellowish, pinkish, to pale red, sometimes quite plain, in others containing irregular streaks of darker colour. The grain is usually straight, but may be shallowly interlocked, and the texture of all types is very fine, dense and smooth.
The timber dries well, is fairly hard to saw, but not difficult to shape and plane. It is classified as being very durable.

Uses
All species have similar uses, piling (not very resistant to *Teredo*), wharf and bridge building, posts, poles, sills, floors, interior finish, window frames, and for furniture and cabinets

ASH, JAPANESE

Fraxinus mandshurica Rupr.   Family: Oleaceae

Other names
tamo.

Distribution
Manchuria, Korea and Japan.

The tree
Attains a height of 18m to 30m and a diameter of 0.75m.

The timber
The sapwood is white, and the heartwood is light brown in colour, darker than European ash, and rather lighter in weight, being about 690 kg/m³ when dried. The grain is straight, sometimes wavy, and the texture is coarse.

Drying
Dries fairly rapidly without much tendency to warp, split or check.

Strength
Although a strong timber for its weight it is generally less strong than European ash, and lacks the characteristic toughness of that timber.

Durability
Perishable.

Working qualities
Fairly easy to work, it has only a moderate dulling effect on cutting edges, and generally works to a good finish. It takes glue, stains, and polish satisfactorily.

Uses
Flooring, plywood, baseball bats, skis, furniture, etc. Selected material furnishes decorative veneer with mottle, fiddle-back and curly-grain features.

Note: This timber should not be confused with sen (*Kalopanax pictus* Nakai. syn. *Acanthopanax recinifolius* Seem.). Although similar in appearance to Japanese ash, it is lighter in weight, about 560 kg/m³ when dried, and has none of the valuable attributes of ash. It is generally used for interior joinery and panelling.

BAMBOO

Although the Gramineae family of plants does not produce timber in the accepted sense, nevertheless, certain genera of this family produce bamboo, a material of extreme economic importance in the Philippines and elsewhere, used for construction or for the manufacture of furniture and implements, and for this reason a brief summary of the most important species is given here.

The erect bamboos are the most abundant and useful, and have cylindrical, hollow stems, with walls ranging from less than 5mm to 40mm or 50mm in thickness. In all species, the walls are thickest at the butt, and become gradually thinner towards the tip. In some species, the wall of the first few joints above the rootstock is so thick that the stems are almost, or quite solid. The erect bamboos have, as a rule, perfectly straight stems.

The following are a few of the most important species of the Philippines.

Bambusa blumeana Schultes f. produces the spiny bamboo, found in all settled areas at low and medium altitudes, and extensively planted. Considered to be the best structural bamboo in the Philippines. Used in house construction, temporary bridges and wharves, fish weirs, and for all purposes where the strongest and most durable bamboo is required.

Bambusa vulgaris Schrad. produces a tall straight bamboo known as kawayan-kiling. Whilst spiny bamboo is preferred for heavy work on account of its greater strength and durability, kawayan-kiling is favoured for furniture, floors, window and door frames.

Schizostachyum dielsianum Merr. produces bikal-babui a general purpose bamboo, used particularly for chairs.

Bamboo is used for a vast range of products, and particularly for the following.

House construction; posts, joists, studding, laths, rafters, purlins, door and window frames, shutters and eave troughs.

General construction; scaffolding and staging, centering for masonry culverts and arches, shade frames for nursery beds and for flag-poles.

11

Land transportation; yokes, vehicle shafts and rollers for moving heavy objects.
Furniture and household equipment; benches, chairs, tables, beds and bookshelves.
Navigation; masts and spars for boats, oar shafts, boat poles, seats and false bottoms, and ribs for boat awnings.

Because of the high yield of cellulose, much bamboo is used for paper pulp.

BANUYO

Wallaceodendron celebicum Koord.   Family: Leguminosae

Other names
derham mahogany (USA).

Distribution
Philippines, mainly from Luzon and Masbate.

The tree
Although a fairly tall tree, the bole is short, and often crooked, with a diameter of 1.5m.

The timber
The sapwood is whitish, up to 30mm wide, and generally sharply defined from the heartwood which varies in colour from light golden-brown to dark brown, sometimes with a distinct reddish tint. The grain is usually straight, but may be interlocked, curly, or wavy, while the texture is fine. The wood has a glossy appearance when planed, and a thin, light-coloured line of parenchyma marks each season's growth. The wood weighs about 528 kg/m^3 when dried. It is said to dry easily and well, to machine without difficulty, and to glue, stain and polish satisfactorily. The wood is moderately durable.

Uses
Furniture, cabinets, doors, window frames, panelling, mouldings, ship cabins, and for musical instruments, particularly for the backs and sides of guitars.

BATETE

Kingiodendron alternifoliium Merr.　　　Family : Leguminosae

Other names
bagbalogo, bahai, bitangol, palomaria.

Distribution
Found from central Luzon to Mindanao; large trees up to
1.0m in diameter, fairly numerous in parts of Masbate, elsewhere scattered.

General characteristics
The sapwood which varies in width from 15mm to 50mm is
pale red at first, turning dull brown in drying, and not very well
distinguished from the heartwood which is light to dark reddish-
brown, with blackish streaks due to oil which exudes and stains
all surfaces. The grain is fairly straight and the texture fine. The
wood is soft to moderately hard, weighs about 704 kg/m³ and
is moderately durable.
Batete needs care in drying in order to avoid warping, but it does
not tend to check unduly.

Uses
Beams, joists, rafters, flooring, doors, interior joinery.

BATICULIN

Litsea obtusata F.-Vill.　　　Family : Lauraceae

Other names
batikuling.

A particular feature of sculpture in the Philippines is the making
of sacred images. Some of these are permanently set up out-
doors, and first choice of timber for this purpose are woods like
molave and merbau. Soft, less durable woods are also used,
but these require annual painting, and preservative treatment
initially, or ultimately, and wood of this type is less favoured.
The principal type used for soft, easy carving, are the yellow
baticulins, of which *Litsea obtusata* appears to be more
regularly used and considered best.

13

The wood of *L. obtusata* has a pale yellow sapwood, up to 30mm wide, not clearly demarcated from the heartwood which is bright golden-yellow when freshly cut, turning darker on exposure. The wood has a faint odour reminiscent of both cedar and camphor. The grain is straight, and the texture fine, and the wood has a smooth, waxy feel, taking a glossy surface under sharp tools. It dries easily and well, and is very easy to work, and weighs about 400 kg/m³ when dried. It is classified as being moderately durable.

Uses
Apart from the carving and sculpture of sacred images, the wood is also used for panelling for altars, doors, musical instruments and cabinets.

BEECH, JAPANESE

Fagus crenata Bl.   Family: Fagaceae
and allied species

Other names
Siebold's beech, buna.

Distribution
Japan.

General characteristics
Very similar in appearance and characteristics to European beech, the sapwood is cream-coloured, the heartwood brown in colour. The grain is straight, and the texture fine, more nearly approaching that of central European beech, than of English. It weighs about 640 kg/m³ when dried, and is therefore lighter than European and American beech.

It is perishable, but accepts preservatives readily, and is used for furniture, flooring, joinery, turnery, plywood, tool handles, and for constructional work, sleepers (treated), and pulp.

BINGGAS

Terminalia citrina (Gaertn.) Roxb.   Family: Combretaceae
syn *T. comintana* Merr.

Distribution
Scattered in the Dipterocarp forests of Luzon, Mindoro, Leyte,

Negros, Mindanao, and elsewhere in the Philippines, and therefore limited in supply.

The tree
Although a large tree with only a moderate buttress, the bole is generally only about 12m to 18m in length, and may be irregular in form. Its diameter is usually about 0.9m.

The timber
The sapwood is light-yellow in colour and between 40mm and 100mm wide, and slightly distinct from the light reddish-yellow heartwood. Timber from large trees frequently contains either dark streaks, or has a violet tint. The grain is shallowly interlocked or slightly crossed, and the texture is moderately fine with a rather glossy appearance. It is a heavy wood, weighing about 910 kg/m^3 when dried.

Drying
Difficult to dry from the green, being prone to checking and warping, and therefore requires great care.

Strength
A strong, hard wood, comparing favourably with hickory in toughness and with many of the Australian *Eucalypts* in general strength.

Durability
Durable.

Working qualities
Fairly difficult to work due to its hard, tough nature, but with care capable of a good smooth finish.

Uses
Frame construction in buildings, and for vehicle bodies. It is favoured locally for tool handles as an alternative to hickory, and in limited tests showed promise as a material for picker sticks in the textile industry.

BIRCH, JAPANESE

Betula maximowicziana Regel   Family : Betuliaceae

Other names
shira-kamba (Japan).

Distribution
The birches are found from the arctic circle to southern France, and throughout North America, Asia, China and Japan. *B. maximowicziana*, and possibly other species, provide Japanese birch.

The tree
Grows to a height of 18m to 21m and a diameter of 0.5m or a little more on good sites.

The timber
There is no clear distinction by colour between sapwood and heartwood, the wood generally being a bright yellowish-red, with a fairly straight grain, and a fine texture. It weighs about 670 kg/m³ when dried.

Drying
Air dries rapidly, with a tendency to warp, and is particularly susceptible to fungus attack unless the piles are well ventilated.

Strength
A hard, tough wood, with strength properties rather better than those of European oak.

Durability
Perishable.

Working qualities
Works and machines well, although there is a tendency for the wood to bind on the saw, and is sometimes difficult to plane to a smooth finish when knots are present. The wood turns well, and can be glued, stained, and polished satisfactorily. It peels well for veneer.

16

Uses

Furniture, interior joinery, decorative veneer. Birch twigs are used for brooms, and for descaling in steel rolling mills. Timber that contains incipient decay (dote), is often used in Japan for fancy articles, the black zone marks providing a decorative medium.

BOXWOOD, JAPANESE

Buxus sempervirens L.   Family: Buxaceae

Other names

asame-tsuge (Japan).

Distribution

The tree is widely distributed from the Far East throughout Asia, Europe and the Mediterranean countries.

The tree

A small tree, some 6m to 9m in height, and a diameter of about 150mm.

The timber

A fine, compact wood of light yellow colour, with a grain that is sometimes straight, but more often irregular, and a fine, even texture. The wood weighs about 930 kg/m^3 when dried.

Drying

Dries very slowly with a pronounced tendency to surface check. Requires care in drying, since the billets also tend to split rather badly. Splitting these down to half-rounds, and careful piling helps avoid degrade, as does soaking the billets in a saturated solution of common salt, but this can only be done if the effect of the salt on saws, cutters, and machine tables is recognised, and allowed for.

Strength

A heavy, hard timber, twice as hard as oak, and 50 per cent stronger in compression along the grain.

Durability

Durable.

Working qualities

Although resistant to sawing it cuts cleanly, and after drying is rather hard to work. A reduction of cutting angle to 20° will reduce the tendency for irregular grain to tear. The wood turns beautifully, and takes stain and polish well.

Uses

Rollers and shuttles in the silk industry, tool handles, pulley-blocks, fancy turnery, chessmen, and engraving blocks, although cherry is generally preferred for this purpose in Japan today since it is cheaper, and more plentiful.

CALAMANSANAY

Neonauclea spp.   Family : Rubiaceae

Some twenty species of the genus *Neonauclea* occur in the Philippines, mostly small to medium-sized trees, and with the exception of slight differences in colour and texture, the wood is very much alike in general character, and is usually sold as calamansanay irrespective of species, although in certain of the islands, local names may also be applied to a given species. The following are some of the best and commonest species used.

Neonauclea calycina Merr. (syn. *Nauclea calycina* Bartl.) produces typical calamansanay of the trade, and is probably the principal source of the commercial classification.
The tree has a diameter of about 0.8m and the wood is a brilliant rose colour when freshly cut, fading to a dull orange colour after drying. The grain is shallowly interlocked, and the texture fine, the wood sometimes being mottled with irregular darker yellowish-brown or orange markings. The wood is durable.

Neonauclea bartlingii Merr. (syn. *Nauclea bartlingii* D.C.) produces lisak, otherwise known as calamansanay.
The wood is almost entirely yellow in colour, with a fine texture.

Neonauclea bernardoi Merr. (syn. *Nauclea bernardoi* Merr.) produces alintatau or bangkal. This has a pale red-coloured wood, with rather larger pores than the usual species, and therefore of coarser texture. While it is found in several of the islands, it does not generally appear in parcels of calamansanay on the Manila market.

Neonauclea media Merr. (syn. *Nauclea media* Havil) produces a wood very similar to that of *N. calycina*, but it is a little lighter in colour, and coarser in texture.

Neonauclea philippinensis Merr. (syn. *Nauclea philippinensis* Vid.) produces tiroron, or calamansanay. This has wood more distinctly brownish in colour than other species, and has a fine texture.

Neonauclea reticulata Merr. (syn. *Nauclea reticulata* Havil.) produces hambabalud, or calamansanay. This species comes from a medium-sized tree of some 0.4m diameter. The wood is light brown in colour with a slight reddish cast, and more streaked with orange or brown markings than most other species.

Neonauclea vidalii Merr. (syn. *Nauclea vidalii* Elm.) produces tikim or calamansanay. This is a fine textured, light reddish-coloured wood, very similar to typical calamansanay.

Weight
The wood of all species is similar in weight, from 640 kg/m^3 to 672 kg/m^3 when dried.

Drying
Rather slow to dry, and plain-sawn material has a tendency to warp rather badly and to develop surface checks.

Working qualities
All species are said to be rather difficult to work and machine, quarter-sawn stock in particular tending to pick up in planing and moulding. A cutting angle of 10° is helpful, and can assist in producing a reasonable finish. The timber tends to split in nailing, but holds screws quite well. It can be stained and polished after suitable preparation.

Uses
Structural applications for posts, beams, rafters, bridge and wharf construction, and for flooring, sills, tool handles, furniture and cabinets.

CALANTAS

Cedrela calantas Merr. & Rolfe.   Family: Meliaceae

Distribution
In the Philippines, two species of *Cedrela*, ie *C. febrifuga* and *C. paucijuga*, are confined to relatively small areas of Mindoro and Leyte, and the principal species, *C. calantas* appears to be widely distributed throughout the islands.

The tree
The trees vary in height from 21m to 30m with a diameter of 1.8m.

The timber
The sapwood is small, pale red in colour, and sharply defined from the light to dark red heartwood. The grain is straight or shallowly interlocked, and the texture is moderately coarse. The wood has a characteristic cedar odour due to an essential oil which sometimes exudes on the surface of the wood as a sticky resin. Soft, and light in weight, it weighs about 448 kg/m³ when dried.

Drying
Dries fairly rapidly and well but care is needed when drying thick material to avoid internal checking and collapse.

Strength
Variable, but roughly equal to American mahogany except in hardness and shear resistance.

Durability
Durable.

Working qualities
Works and machines readily, but sharp cutting edges must be maintained in order to obtain the best finish because of the soft, and sometimes woolly nature of the timber. Gum is sometimes a problem, but with care, and suitably filled, the wood stains and polishes excellently.

Uses

Cigar boxes, pianos, paddles and light oars, boats and ship's cabin finish, joinery, carving, furniture.

Curly, or bird's-eye calantas, otherwise known as maranggo in the Philippines, is the product of an associated species, ie *Azadirachta integrifolia* Merr. The wood is slightly harder and heavier than calantas, and has the same uses, except for cigar boxes, for which purposes, maranggo is considered to be too dark in colour.

CHERRY, JAPANESE

Prunus spp.   Family : Rosaceae

Other names

yama- zakura (Japan).

General characteristics

The wood is pale pinkish-brown in colour, turning a pleasant mahogany-red on exposure or with polishing. The grain is usually straight, and the texture fine and even. weight about 630 kg/m³ when dried. The wood dries readily, but is inclined to warp. The wood turns well, but a cutting angle of 20° gives the best results in planing. It can be glued and stained, and takes an excellent polish.

Uses

Cabinets, turnery, domestic ware, engraving blocks.

DIOSPYROS SPECIES

The Ebenaceae family includes some thirty or more species of the genus *Diospyros*, providing commercial ebony and persimmon timber. A number of these species occur in the Philippines, where the timber can be roughly grouped into five types, but with two of the groups being the most favoured for high-class work such as furniture and cabinet making and known under the names ebony and camagon respectively.

Segregation of the species into groups is made according to the colour and character of the sapwood, which is generally very wide, the heartwood of all types varying from jet black to blackish, frequently with lighter-coloured streaks. The grouping is as follows,

1 sapwood pinkish or pale red :— camagon group.
2 sapwood with distinct yellowish tint, becoming light yellowish-brown in drying:— heartwood good commercial camagon.
3 Sapwood whitish or dull light grey:— ebony or batulinau group.
4 Sapwood almost white, turning yellowish in drying:— ata-ata group.
5 Sapwood almost white or with a faint reddish tinge, but almost invariably changing shortly after felling to an even bluish-grey:— kanomoi group.

CAMAGON GROUP

The best known and one of the largest trees of the genus is *Diospyros discolor* Willd. the principal species providing camagon. The tree is generally about 0.6m in diameter, the sapwood is up to 200mm wide, generally retaining its pinkish or reddish colour, although fungal staining may introduce a dull grey appearance. The heartwood is sometimes almost dead black, but may be streaked with pink, yellow, brown or greyish colour.

Other species in this group are,
D. copelandii Merr. also known as talang-gubat. This has a diameter of about 0.3m and timber similar to camagon.
D. pilosanthera Blco. also known as bolong-eta. This has a diameter of 0.4m and a wider sapwood than *D. discolor*, but the small heartwood core is identical to that of camagon.
D. plicata Merr. and *D. whitfordii* Merr. produce tamil or palo negro ; both are about 0.3m in diameter, with a small heartwood core similar to camagon.

The principal species forming Group 2 are, *D. philippinensis* A.DC. and *D. velascoi* Merr. The former species is known locally as bolong-eta, or kanumai, and both are fairly small trees with a diameter of about 0.3m.
Apart from the difference in colour of the sapwood, the heartwood core in both species is very similar to camagon.

BATULINAU GROUP

The commonest Philippine name for many of the *Diospyros* species is batulinau, batlatinau, or bulatinau, in the same way that the Spanish name ebano is similarly, and loosely applied. More properly, batulinau or ebony is the product of a single species, *D. buxifolia* Pers. syn. *Maba buxifolia* Pers. This tree is widely distributed throughout the Philippines, but is scattered, with the majority being small trees. Good specimens have a diameter of about 0.4m.

The heartwood is jet black, sometimes with whitish or greyish streaks, and the wood is very hard, very dense and rather brittle.

ATA-ATA GROUP

D. mindanaensis Merr. is one of the largest and most widely distributed, and probably the best known of this group, so that the wood of other species, when its origin is unknown, is generally called ata-ata.

D. mindanaensis; ata-ata, anang, bolong-eta, or tamil-lalaki, has a diameter up to 0.5m and a dark, blackish heartwood generally streaked or mottled with lighter-coloured zones.

D. ahernii Merr. produces anang or ata-ata.

D. alvarezii Merr. produces bantulinau.

D. curranii Merr. produces malagaitmon.

D. foveo-reticulata Merr. produces kulitom or palo negro.

All have similar heartwood.

KANOMOI GROUP

D.multiflora Blco. syn. *D. canomoi* A.DC. is a tree up to 0.6m in diameter, and is the principal source of commercial kanomoi.

D. camarinensis Merr. produces kanumai.

D. maritima Bl. produces malatinta, or kanomoi.

D. nitida Merr. produces katilma or malatinta.

Weight

The weight of the various species differs according to the species and degree of sapwood present, but is generally within the range of 800 kg/m³ to 1040 kg/m³ after drying.

Uses

The segregation of the various species according to the character of the sapwood is relevant to certain uses. Musical instrument

23

manufacturers favour the blue-grey sapwood of the kanomoi group, usually sold under the name malatinta, for backs, sides and finger boards of guitars, while camagon and bolong-eta sapwood, said to be fine, hard, smooth and tough, is used for tool handles.

Camagon sapwood is also used for small show-cases, mouldings, etc while that of all the *Diospyros* species is used in agricultural machinery and implements for parts subjected to severe wear, and for levers, connecting rods and long handles, where rather long or slender working parts require straight grained, fairly tough and springy wood.

The sapwood of bolong-eta (*D. pilosanthera*) is also used for butcher blocks and, along with ata-ata and camagon, for billiard cues. All types are used for shuttles, bobbins and golf-clubs.

The heartwood of all species, and sometimes sapwood and heartwood combined, has a variety of uses both in the high-class, and utility field, including furniture, veneer, cabinet making, turnery, inlaying, paper weights, gun stocks, bank fittings and musical instruments.

HOPEA SPECIES

The family Dipterocarpaceae includes some ten or more species of the genus *Hopea* which produce such timbers as merawan of Malaysia, thingan of Burma and Thailand, and selangan batu of Sabah. Certain species occurring in the Philippines fall into two groups and produce commercial yacal and mangachapuy, the yacals being harder, heavier, and stronger than the mangachapuys, and also more durable.

The following are the principal species forming the two groups.

YACAL

Hopea basilanica Foxw., *H. philippinensis* Dyer., and *H. plagata* Vid.

Other names
dalingdingan, gisok-gisok, banutan, siakal.

General characteristics
Sapwood 20mm to 80mm wide, pale yellow in colour when freshly sawn, but often greyish due to sap-stain, rather sharply distinguished from the heartwood which is light yellowish-brown, darkening rapidly on exposure; sometimes with narrow, irregular greenish streaks which in drying turn greenish-black. The grain is interlocked, making the wood difficult to split radially and producing a sharp ribbon-figure on quarter-sawn surfaces, and the texture is fine and dense, giving the wood a translucent appearance.

The timber is hard to very hard, tough and very stiff, and weighs about 880 kg/m³ when dried. It is said to be very durable when used in contact with the ground.

Yacal needs careful drying; it is not prone to checking but tends to warp badly. It is rather hard to saw and machine, but is capable of a very clean surface off the saw.

Uses
All high-grade permanent construction, except salt water piling; posts, beams, joists, rafters, bridges, wharves, ship framing and decking, flooring, axe and cant-hook handles, sleepers, paving blocks, and wheelwright's work.

Note: a few species of *Vatica* and *Shorea*, principally *S. balangeran*, with similar characteristics are also included in commercial yacal.

MANGACHAPUY

Hopea acuminata Merr., *H. foxworthyi* Elm., and *H. pierrei* Hance.

Other names
bangoran, manggasinoro, barosingsing.

General characteristics
Sapwood 40mm to 80mm wide, lighter in colour than the heartwood which is pale straw colour turning rapidly to clear brown, often with irregular, narrow streaks, grass-green in colour when freshly sawn, but turns to dark greenish-brown or nearly black. The grain is interlocked, but never so strongly as in the yacals,

and there is a small, but attractive ray figure on quarter-sawn surfaces. The texture is fine to very fine, and the wood weighs from 590 kg/m³ to 725 kg/m³ when dried.

Mangachapuy is easy to dry without excessive degrade, easy to work and machine, and capable of a good, smooth finish in planing and moulding. The wood is moderately durable.

Uses
Posts, beams, rafters, flooring, sheathing, masts, spars, planking and decking for boats, doors, mouldings, pestle shafts in rice mills, furniture, cabinets, broom, rake and hoe handles.

HORSE CHESTNUT, JAPANESE

Aesculus turbinata Bl.   Family : Hippocastanaceae

Other names
tochi, tochi-noki (Japan).

Distribution
Found in Japan principally in the Chuenji district.

The tree
Grows to a height of 30m or more, and a diameter of 1.5m. The bole length is generally short, about 6m to 8m in length.

The timber
There is little distinction by colour between sapwood and heartwood, the wood generally being a golden-brown colour, darker than European horse chestnut. The grain is wavy or crossed, and the texture fine and uniform, and the wood is a little heavier than the European variety, weighing about 590 kg/m³ when dried.

Drying
Dries readily and without excessive degrade.

Strength
No information.

Durability
Perishable.

Working qualities

Works and machines without undue difficulty, although inclined to woolliness. Thin-edged, sharp cutters produce a very good finish, and the wood can be glued, stained and polished without difficulty. It is a good turnery timber.

Uses

Selected logs containing mottle figure, and especially those containing incipient decay, ie with yellowish patches of discoloured wood enclosed by black zone markings, are prized in Japan for decorative work. Normal stock is used for domestic utensils, food containers and fruit storage trays.

KAKI

Diospyros kaki L.f.   Family: Ebenaceae

Other names

Chinese persimmon.

Distribution

The genus *Diospyros* produces the true ebonies, and also includes a few species which are fruit-bearing, and unlike the ebonies, usually have a very wide, straw-coloured and commercial sapwood, and a comparatively small black core of heartwood. These are the persimmons, of which *D. virginiana* produces persimmon of North America, and *D. kaki* produces very similar wood, mainly from Japan. *D. lotus* L. produces the date plum of temperate Asia, but this is known more for its fruit rather than for its timber.

General characteristics

Anatomically, there is very little difference between kaki and American persimmon, but in many of the Japanese trees, the dark heartwood is often much wider than that found in the American species. The heartwood is basically dense black, but usually streaked with orange-yellow, brown, grey or salmon-pink, separately, or in combination, giving a highly decorative appearance to the wood, which has a cold, marble-like feel on planed surfaces. It is lighter in weight than ebony, weighing 768 kg/m³ when dried.

Uses
Highly-prized in Japan for ornamental work and small tables, the straw-coloured sapwood is used for golf-club heads, turnery, textile shuttles, and any work demanding a close, compact wood with an ability to wear smooth.

KATSURA

Cercidiphyllum japonicum   Family : Trochodendraceae
Sieb. & Zucc.

Distribution
Japan.

General characteristics
A deciduous hardwood tree, it tends to form several furrowed trunks, often spirally twisted.

The timber is of a light nut-brown colour, rather plain in appearance but with an occasional narrow, light-coloured line due to growth rings which are marked by a narrow band of parenchyma. The wood somewhat resembles American white-wood (*Liriodendron*), with its rather crowded, small pores and parenchyma, but katsura is a little more brown in colour.

Logs selected for timber are usually straight-grained, and the texture is fine and even. The wood is soft but compact, and light in weight, about 470 kg/m^3 when dried.

The timber dries easily and well, and is very easy to work and machine, its soft, yet compact nature lending itself to moulding and carving where there is a need for sharp arrises to remain intact and not chip out.

Uses
Furniture, cabinets, panelling, high-class joinery, mouldings, carving, engraving.

KEYAKI

Zelkova serrata Makino.   Family : Ulmaceae
syn. *Z. acuminata* Planch.

Distribution
Of several species of *Zelkova*, two are important, *Z. carpinifolia*

syn. *Z. crenata*, found in Iran and the Caucasus, and *Z. serrata*, syn. *Z. acuminata*. a native of China and Japan. Both species have been introduced into the UK.

The tree
Z. serrata attains a height of 36m and a diameter of 1.2m. The bole is smooth and straight in young trees, but progressively becomes deeply fissured, and in old trees has the appearance of a number of boles, fused together.

The timber
Zelkova is closely related to the elms, and the timber is not unlike elm in appearance. The wood is yellowish-brown in colour when freshly cut, turning a lustrous golden colour after drying, but lighter in colour than elm. The wood is ring porous, with a similar undulating arrangement of late-wood pores as in elm. The timber is a little heavier than elm and weighs about 625 kg/m^3 when dried, and is said to be very resistant to decay.

Uses
A strong, tough, and elastic wood, it is used in China and Japan at the present time mainly for the building and maintenance of temples, and is largely a protected tree, reserved for this purpose. The tree is capable of great age, and due to the particular form, and also to its capacity to produce very large burrs, highly decorative wood can be obtained, but while for centuries the wood was used for lacquer work, cabinets, carving, and highly polished columns in temples, very old trees, 1000 years old, it is said, became scarce, and for a long time now its use has been restricted, at least in Japan.

KIRI

Paulownia tomentosa C. Koch.   Family: Scrophulariaceae
syn *P. imperialis* Sieb. & Zucc.

Other name
foxglove tree (UK).

Distribution
Two species of *Paulownia* are of relative economic importance

ie *P. fargesii* which occurs in China, and *P. tomentosa*, which is found in Japan, and which was introduced into the UK from Japan in 1838.

The tree
Kiri is a fairly small tree some 15m to 18m in height, with a diameter of 0.6m or a little more.

General characteristics
The wood varies in colour, from silver-grey, to light brown, sometimes with a reddish cast. It is very light in weight, about 320 kg/m^3 when dried. The wood is very highly prized in Japan for a wide range of products, from cabinets and drawer linings, to musical instruments, clogs, and floats for fishing nets. It is also used to produce scale-veneer, which is of extreme thinness, and this is often mounted on paper to produce special visiting cards, particularly from the silver-grey coloured wood.

LANIPAU

Terminalia copelandi Elm. Family: Combretaceae
syn. *T. crassiramea* Merr.

Distribution
This species appears to be confined to Leyte and Mindanao, especially in Agusan and Davao.

The tree
A medium-sized tree with a clear cylindrical bole of 8m to 10m and a diameter of 0.6m to 0.8m.

The timber
The sapwood is yellowish-brown, not much differentiated from the heartwood, which is reddish-brown, or pinkish-brown in colour. The grain is interlocked and sometimes wavy, and the texture is moderately coarse. The timber weighs about 561 kg/m^3 when dried.

Drying
Moderately difficult to dry, with similar drying characteristics to those of bagtikan, mayapis and tangile.

Strength
Moderately strong, and similar to almon in general strength, but this would seem of little consequence since the timber is seldom used for structural purposes.

Durability
Non-durable.

Working qualities
Works and machines fairly well, but its coarse nature tends to promote a rather poor finish in planing. It peels quite well, producing a core-stock veneer.

Uses
General construction and roofing shingles.

LAUAN

Shorea, Parashorea and
Pentacme species

Family: Dipterocarpaceae

The Dipterocarpaceae is by far the most important botanical family in the Philippines, at least half of the standing timber belonging to it. The trees are almost without exception tall and straight, and their timber is utilized for a wider range of uses than those of any other family.

While there is a very wide range of weight, hardness, colour, and mechanical properties, as well as durability, there are certain features of structure that are fairly uniform throughout the whole family, from the softest of the lauans to the hardest of the yacals. Growth rings are rare, except in the first years of growth, ripple marks are rarer still, and when present, rather indistinct. The most characteristic feature of the timbers of this family is the presence of numerous resin ducts, partly scattered, but more often arranged in conspicuous narrow concentric lines, giving the appearance of growth rings.

The lauans consist of various species of *Shorea, Parashorea,* and *Pentacme,* and correspond roughly to the merantis of Malaysia and seraya of Sabah. In the Philippines it is the usual practice to classify the timbers into two groups on the basis of colour, ie the darker coloured timbers as red or dark red lauan, and the whitish or pale-coloured timbers as light red or white lauan.

In some cases, an individual species is sold under a separate trade name, for example, *Shorea polysperma* may be marketed as tangile, but may also be included in parcels of red lauan. Furthermore, some species vary in colour, and may provide timber for both groups.

The principal species providing lauan are as follows,
Red lauan ; *Shorea negrosensis* Foxw. (red lauan proper),
Dark red lauan ; *S. negrosensis* Foxw ; *S. polysperma* Merr.; *S. squamata* Dyer syn *S. palosapis* Merr. (in part) ; *S. agsaboensis* Stern. Some, or all of these species may be included as red lauan.
White lauan or light red lauan includes *Parashorea malaanonan* (Blco.) Merr.; *Shorea almon* Foxw., selected material of *S. squamata*, and species of *Pentacme*, of which *P. contorta* Merr. provides white lauan proper, and *P. mindanensis* Foxw. produces Mindanao white lauan.

The following are descriptions of the various species making up the lauans, with particular reference to those sold under separate trade names.

RED LAUAN

Shorea negrosensis Foxw.

Other name
Philippine mahogany (UK). This name is confusing and its use should be discontinued.

Distribution
Occurs widely in the Philippines, especially in Cagayan, Isabela, Laguna, Quezon, Negros provinces, Northern Mindanao and Bucas Grande Island.

The tree
A large tree, some 50m tall with a diameter of 2m. It is strongly buttressed, with a straight, cylindrical bole, slightly tapered.

Clear boles of 20m are common, and on good sites can reach 30m.

The timber
The sapwood is about 50mm wide, creamy or light grey in colour, and sharply defined from the reddish to dark red heartwood. It has a crossed or interlocked grain, showing a distinct ribbon-grain pattern on quarter-sawn surfaces. Weight about 630 kg/m³ when dried.

Drying
Dries easily and with little degrade.

Strength
Generally the strength of red lauan compares closely with that of American mahogany, but it is less hard, and rather weaker in compression strength parallel to the grain.

Durability
Moderately durable.

Working qualities
Works easily with both hand and machine tools, and is capable of a good finish in planing and moulding, although it is sometimes essential to reduce cutting angles to 20° to avoid grain tearing. Takes stains and polish well and glues satisfactorily. Peels well for veneer.

Uses
Red lauan, as with other lauan types, is a general utility wood. It is however, widely used as peeler and veneer log; furniture, interior finish and panelling, planking and decking of boats, and for cabinets and cases of musical and scientific instruments.

WHITE LAUAN

Pentacme contorta Merr.

Distribution
Widely distributed in the Philippine Islands, in association with other white lauans and apitong.

The tree
A large tree attaining a height of 45m to 50m and a diameter of 1.8m.

The timber
The sapwood is 50mm to 90mm wide, light grey in colour, while the heartwood is also greyish with a reddish tinge, or light pink. The grain is interlocked, sometimes crossed, and the texture is moderately coarse. The resin ducts are in concentric arcs, and are filled with white resin. Weight about 530 kg/m^3 when dried.

Drying
Dries easily and well. Shrinkage, from green to 12 per cent moisture content 4.3 per cent tangentially, 1.8 per cent radially.

Strength
Comparable, or a little superior, to the general strength properties of American mahogany (*Swietenia* spp.), but slightly inferior in hardness and impact resistance.

Durability
Moderately durable.

Working qualities
White lauan works and machines easily and finishes quite well in planing and moulding. There is a tendency for the wood to tear in boring and mortising. It peels well, and takes glue, stains and polish satisfactorily.

Uses
Veneer, plywood, furniture, cabinets, interior joinery, boat planking.

ALMON

Shorea almon Foxw.

Distribution
Widely distributed in the Philippines in primary forests where there is no pronounced dry season, usually in association with other white lauans and apitong.

The tree
A large tree, reaching a height of 70m and a diameter of 1.6m. The bole is almost cylindrical and evenly tapered and is usually clear for 25m to 30m.

The timber
The sapwood is cream to light brown in colour, not sharply demarcated from the reddish to light brown heartwood. It is intermediate in colour between the red and white lauans, although in some regions it could pass for red lauan. The resin ducts are filled with white resin and it is comparatively light in weight, about 580 kg/m^3 when dried.

Drying
Said to be the easiest to dry of all the species in the lauan groups. Shrinkage from green to 12 per cent moisture content is 5.6 per cent tangentially and 2.8 per cent radially.

Strength
The strength properties of this timber compare closely with those of bagtikan; by comparison with American mahogany its strength in bending, compression and stiffness is superior to mahogany, but it is slightly inferior to that timber in hardness and impact resistance.

Durability
Moderately durable.

Working qualities
Works quite well in most machine operations but the grain tends to tear in shaping, turning, and boring It can be planed to a smooth finish and takes glue, stains and polish, satisfactorily, It peels well for veneer.

Uses
Veneer, plywood, furniture, interior finish and panelling, boat planking and decking and as structural members in light frame construction.

BAGTIKAN

Parashorea malaanonan (Bclo) Merr. Syn. *P. plicata* Brandis

Distribution
Occurs in the Philippines in some parts of Luzon, in Polilio, Mindanao, Biliran, Catanduanes, Negros, Masbate.

The tree
Attains a height of 50m to 60m and a diameter of 1.0m. The cylindrical bole is usually about 20m to 25m in length.

The timber
Bagtikan is of the light red lauan type; the sapwood is 20mm to 30mm wide, light grey in colour and not sharply defined from the heartwood which is greyish-brown and often with light-brown concentric bands which are spaced some 50mm to 100mm apart. The grain is usually crossed and the texture is moderately coarse. The wood is moderately heavy, weighing about 530 kg/m^3 when dried.

Drying
Rather difficult to dry, it has a marked tendency to check and warp and is susceptible to collapse. Air drying to 25 per cent moisture content prior to kiln drying is recommended. Shrinkage from the green to 12 per cent moisture content is 5.7 per cent tangentially, and 3.5 per cent radially.

Strength
Among the lauans, bagtikan is the strongest timber, excelling them all in general strength properties. It is superior to American mahogany (*Swietenia*) in stiffness (modulus of elasticity), impact resistance and toughness and compares very closely to mahogany in all other strength properties.

Durability
Moderately durable.

Working qualities
Rather hard to work and rather difficult to shape, but it planes well and takes glue, stains and polish satisfactorily. It also peels well for veneer.

Uses
For domestic consumption bagtikan is usually mixed with white lauan, almon and mayapis and used for house construction,

veneer, plywood, furniture and interior joinery. Bagtikan is usually included in shipments of light red lauan.

GUIJO

Shorea guiso Bl.   Family: Dipterocarpaceae

Other names
red balau (Malaysia) ; red selangan batu (Sabah).

Distribution
Found throughout S E Asia and throughout the Philippines.

General characteristics
The tree is large, up to 1.8m in diameter, and the timber is moderately heavy to heavy, weighing from 817 kg/m³ to 880 kg/m³ when dried.

The sapwood is up to 50mm wide, light greyish-brown in colour, not sharply defined from the heartwood which is light greyish brown to brown, sometimes with a distinct reddish tint. The grain is interlocked, and the texture coarse, but even. The wood dries slowly, and needs care if warping and splitting is to be avoided. Resin ducts appear as frequent narrow rings.
The wood saws easily, but is rather difficult to shape and plane to a good finish.

Uses
Beams, joists, rafters, flooring, windows, doors, keels, planking and decking for boats, piling, except salt water, vehicle parts, bridge and wharf construction.

MAYAPIS

Shorea squamata Dyer.

Distribution
Abundant in primary forests of the Philippines at low and medium altitudes, particularly in Luzon, Polilio, Leyte, Mindanao and Basilan island.

The tree
A medium-size tree with a large buttress, it reaches a height of

40m or a little more, and a diameter of 1.5m with a clear bole 20m to 30m in length.

The timber
A light-red lauan type, the sapwood is 25mm to 50mm wide, pinkish in colour, and gradually merging into the reddish heartwood. The colour of the heartwood is variable; from some localities it is sufficiently red to pass as tangile or red lauan, while in other areas it is light-red, and is marketed as white lauan. The grain is crossed or interlocked, and the texture is moderately coarse to coarse. The resin ducts are usually empty. The wood is comparatively light in weight, about 530 kg/m³ when dried.

Drying
Variable in drying properties according to locality of growth. Timber from N and S E Luzon is moderately slow drying, with minor degrade developing in the form of checking and warping. Timber from N E Mindanao is said to dry much more slowly, especially from sinker logs which have a high green moisture content. This type of timber needs very careful drying if severe checking, warping and collapse is to be avoided.

Air drying to 25 per cent moisture content prior to kiln drying is recommended, otherwise a very mild kiln schedule should be employed when drying from the green. Shrinkage, green to 12 per cent moisture content is said to be 6.4 per cent tangentially, and 4.4 per cent radially.

Strength
Similar to almon in all strength categories.

Durability
Moderately durable.

Working qualities
Works readily, planes very well, but is poor in shaping, turning, boring and mortising. Peeling and gluing properties are good, but veneers are sometimes difficult to dry.

Uses
Furniture, cabinets, cigar boxes, veneer and plywood, boat planking and general construction.

TANGILE

Shorea polysperma Merr.

Distribution
The tree is widely distributed in high-altitude forest regions of the Philippines.

The tree
A large tree, reaching a height of 45m to 50m and a diameter of 2m and with a bole length of 25m to 33m.

The timber
The sapwood is 40mm to 50mm wide, creamy in colour and sharply defined from the red to dark brownish-red heartwood. The grain is crossed or interlocked, showing a distinct ribbon-grain figure on quarter-sawn surfaces. The texture is somewhat fine, and the wood has a slight lustre, is moderately hard, and comparatively light, weighing about 630 kg/m^3 when dried.

Drying
Moderately slow drying, it has a tendency to warp, and for wide, plain-sawn boards to cup, and accordingly, proper attention must be given to the spacing of sticks, which should be fairly close, while weighting down of stacks is recommended.

Strength
Very similar in all strength properties to red lauan (*S. negrosensis*).

Durability
Moderately durable.

Working qualities
Works well with all hand tools, but requires care in planing and moulding, particularly when planing quarter-sawn material, to avoid grain tearing. It turns, peels, glues, stains and polishes satisfactorily.

Uses
Tangile to some extent resembles true mahogany and for that reason has similar uses for furniture, cabinet making, joinery

such as sash-frames, doors and interior finish. It is used widely for boat planking, veneer, plywood, and for general construction.

TIAONG

Shorea agsaboensis Stern

Distribution
Found in abundance in Laguna and Quezon in the Philippines and also in low-altitude primary forests where there is abundant rainfall.

The tree
Tiaong reaches a height of 20m and a diameter of 1.75m.

The timber
Very similar to tangile in general appearance, but generally lighter in colour. It has few resin ducts which look like numerous broken lines on end-grain surfaces, whereas in tangile they appear as definite solid lines. Tiaong weighs about 630 kg/m^3 when dried.

Drying
No work has been carried out on this species, but it is believed to have similar drying characteristics to almon.

Strength
Similar to tangile and red lauan in general strength properties, but lower in stiffness.

Durability
Perishable.

Uses
General house construction locally, and for furniture, veneer and plywood.

LIUSIN

Parinarium corymbosum Miq.   Family: Rosaceae

Distribution
Widely, but sparsely distributed throughout the Philippines.

General characteristics

The tree has a diameter of 0.6m although larger specimens are found occasionally. The wood is hard and heavy, weighing about 1120 kg/m³ when dried.

The wood is pale red in colour, sometimes streaked with very narrow, widely separated, dark belts of colour which do not generally follow the growth rings. The grain is straight, or slightly crossed, often with a characteristic regular wave, while the texture is fine; the wood has a faint acid odour.

The timber dries slowly and without much checking, but it is said to warp rather badly.

Difficult to work, blunting cutting edges rapidly, but with suitable techniques can be finished quite well.

Uses

Although said to be only moderately durable in respect of timber in contact with the ground, it has a high reputation for resistance to *Teredo*, and is favoured for piling in salt water. It is used for boat keels, railway ties (preservative treated), and when planing difficulties are overcome makes splendid flooring.

There is a further species, *P. laurinum* A. Gray occurring in the islands, known as tabon-tabon. This wood is practically identical to liusin, but the tree is smaller, up to 0.4m in diameter.

MALABAYABAS

Tristania decorticata Merr.   Family: Myrtaceae

Other names

Similar timber is produced by *T. littoralis* Merr. and is known as taba, while a few unclassified species produce tiga.

General characteristics

The wood of all the species is very hard and heavy, weighing around 1200 kg/m³ when dried. The sapwood is up to 30mm wide, light brown in colour, merging gradually into the heartwood which is dark brown, turning almost black after long exposure. The grain is shallowly interlocked, and the texture fine and glossy. White deposits occur in many of the pores.

With care, the wood dries quite well, but there is a tendency for warping and checking to develop. Fairly hard to work, but it can be planed to a good finish with care.

41

Uses
Very durable, the three species mentioned are used for piling, bridge and wharf construction, posts, sills, joists and rafters. Taba and tiga appear to be used under their own names but malabayabas, while also used for these purposes often as a substitute for mancono, although for specialist uses it is inferior to mancono.

MALAGAI

Pometia pinnata Forst.   Family : Sapindaceae

Other names
malugay, agupanga (Philippines) ; taun (Papua New Guinea) ; kasai (Solomons).

Distribution
A single species, widely distributed throughout the South Pacific.

The tree
The tree reaches a height of 36m to 45m with a diameter of 1.0m above the buttress.

The timber
The sapwood is 30mm to 50mm wide, pale reddish in colour, and not clearly distinguished from the heartwood which is pale pinkish-brown darkening with age. There appears to be some variation in colour in the timber from different localities in the Philippines, some having a light red heartwood, while much grown in Mindanao is dark reddish-brown. The grain may be straight, but more usually it is interlocked, with a characteristic regular wave, while the texture is fine and smooth, although this may not apply to timber from all localities since the wood grown in Papua New Guinea is said to have a coarse and uneven texture. Weight about 750 kg/m^3 when dried.

Drying
Dries reasonably well, but care must be taken to avoid warping and checking.

Strength
The strength properties are similar to those of European beech.

Durability
Moderately durable.

Working qualities
Works and machines fairly well, with only a moderate blunting effect on cutting edges. With attention to techniques a good finish can be obtained in planing and moulding. The wood takes glue and the normal finishing treatments satisfactorily.

Uses
Where fairly abundant in the Philippines the wood is well-known and favoured for beams, joists, rafters, flooring, ceilings and interior trim, furniture, cabinets, levers, capstan bars, minor tool handles, and masts and spars in boat building. Australian tests on taun, the Papua New Guinea equivalent, indicate good peeling properties for veneer. Mindoro appears to have the most abundant supply.

MANCONO

Xanthostemon verdugonianus Naves.   Family : Myrtaceae

Other names
palo de hierro, Philippine ironwood, Philippine lignum vitae.

Distribution
The tree is generally scarce in the Philippines, except in Surigao in the north of Mindanao.

The tree
The tree attains a fair height, but the bole is generally very short, branches often starting 1m or 2m from the ground, although in exceptionally good trees the bole may be up to 10m clear of branches. Diameters vary from 0.3m to 1m.

The timber
The local names of ironwood and lignum vitae are more descriptive of the character of the wood rather than on a botanical relationship, although mancono is related to ironbark of Australia.
Despite the relatively small saw-logs, the timber is a valuable

local material, substituting for lignum vitae in many traditional uses. Mancono wood is very hard, and very heavy, weighing about 1280 kg/m³ when dried, a little heavier than lignum vitae.

The sapwood is from 10mm to 20mm wide, pale red in colour, sharply defined from the heartwood which is yellowish-brown when freshly cut, turning to a dark bronze after drying, and almost black with age. The grain is always crossed, frequently curly and twisted, but the texture is extremely fine and dense, to the extent that bare wood can be burnished almost like metal, due to the few, and very small pores scattered in the wood, the very fine rays, and the fact that soft parenchyma tissue is practically absent.

Drying
Large logs often contain radial heart cracks, but sawn material although drying extremely slowly, tends only to check superficially and not deeply.

Durability
Very durable. It is said that small logs used as posts have only about 10mm of decayed sapwood after 40 years in the ground, and similar stock used for salt water piling is only similarly degraded due to teredo attack after 20 years.

Uses
The wood is extremely difficult to work, but it is used locally for pulleys, rollers, bowling balls, dumb-bells, bearings, saw-guide blocks, tool handles, novelties, paper weights, posts and piles.

MAPLE, JAPANESE

Acer mono Maxim. et al.   Family : Aceraceae

A number of species of *Acer* produce maple, and it is probable that more than one provides commercial maple timber of Japan, but since this is generally of uniform character, it is also probable that some distinctions are made in the selection from the many species found in Japan, *A. mono* appears to be a principal species, along with *A. palmatum*.

General characteristics
A light-coloured wood, with grain usually straight, but occasionally wavy. The creamy white sapwood is not sharply defined from the heartwood, which however, generally has a reddish tinge. The texture is fine and even, and the growth rings produce fine brown lines on longitudinal surfaces. The wood is very similar in appearance to rock maple (*A. saccharum*), but is a little lighter in weight, about 670 kg/m³ when dried.

Uses
Used as an alternative to rock maple for furniture, panelling, cabinets, flooring, for bowling alleys, dance-halls, warehouses, squash courts, and for decorative veneer.

MENGKULANG

Heritiera javanica Bl.   Family: Sterculiaceae

Other names
lumbayao, gisang.

Distribution
A number of species of *Heritiera* occur in the tropics, including niangon of West Africa, and chumprak of Thailand. *H. javanica* is the principal species found in the Philippines.

The tree
A fairly large tree, some 36m tall, with a diameter of 0.6m and a generally straight and cylindrical bole above the buttress.

The timber
The sapwood is pale yellowish-red in colour, merging gradually into the light red to reddish-brown heartwood, the wood from medium-sized trees resembling cigar-box cedar, and the darker-coloured wood being more like African mahogany in appearance. The grain is straight or interlocked, sometimes wavy, producing a stripe figure on quarter-sawn surfaces, while a fine fleck figure is also present, due to the rather large rays. The texture is open and rather coarse, and the wood has a greasy feel. It weighs about 720 kg/m³ when dried, and is moderately durable.

Drying
The timber dries fairly rapidly, without excessive degrade, there being only a mild tendency to splitting, warping and checking.

Strength
Similar to teak, but large trees often contain brittleheart.

Working qualities
Works and machines with moderate ease, but tends to blunt tools, especially saw teeth, fairly quickly. Quarter-sawn stock tends to pick up in planing and moulding and a reduction of cutting angle to 15° is helpful in obtaining a good finish. The pores contain a red gum which sometimes tends to interfere with polishing, but this can be overcome with care.

Uses
Used locally for furniture, cabinets, flooring, doors, interior finish, boat ribs and planking.

A wood known as lumbayao batu also occurs in the Philippines, but this is very hard, heavy, and darker in colour, and is less favoured. Generally used for constructional purposes, its botanical origin is obscure.

MERBAU

Intsia bijuga O. Ktze.   Family : Leguminosae

Other names
ipil (Philippines) ; kwila (Papua New Guinea) ; hintzy (Madagascar).

Distribution
Intsia bijuga occurs throughout the South-west Pacific Islands, Madagascar, and the Philippines, while *I. palembanica* is found in Malaysia and Indonesia.

The tree
Merbau is a tall, straight tree, up to 1.8m in diameter.

The timber

The sapwood is 40mm to 80mm wide, whitish, and sharply distinguished from the heartwood, which when fresh, is bright yellow, turning dark brown on exposure. Lighter-coloured parenchyma usually gives an ornamental figure on tangential surfaces. The wood has an oily odour, and small quantities of oil exuding from the surface cause characteristic small, dull black spots to occur on planed surfaces.

The grain is straight, but may be interlocked, and the texture coarse but even. The wood weighs about 900 kg/m³ when dried.

Drying

The timber dries slowly, and requires care in order to avoid surface checking, particularly in thick dimensions.

Strength

No information, but it is reputed to be a good, strong wood.

Durability

Durable.

Working qualities

Rather hard to saw, the gum clogging saw teeth quite rapidly. A reduction of cutting angle to 20° in planing and moulding helps to reduce the tendency for grain to tear, especially in quarter-sawn material. The wood tends to split in nailing, but it holds screws well, and with care, can be stained and polished.

Uses

All high-class general construction, posts, beams, joists, rafters, transmission poles, sills, ties, flooring, siding, sheathing, doors and windows, ship, wharf, and bridge building, except salt water piling, agricultural implements.

The sulphur-yellow deposits in the pores are soluble in water and the dye thus produced can have a lasting effect on textiles or fair faced concrete, where these are used in contact with wet wood.

MOLAVE

Vitex parviflora Juss.   Family: Verbenaceae

Distribution

About nine species of the genus *Vitex* occur in the Philippines, but only about two are widely distributed or well-known, one of these, *V. aherniana* Merr. produces a timber known as sasalit, a very durable species with a high resistance to marine borer attack, but of limited availability, and the best known is *V. parviflora*, or molave.

The tree
A large tree with a diameter of 2m or more, but with a short, fluted bole.

The timber
The sapwood is small and not clearly distinct from the heart-wood, which is pale straw-colour to light brown, sometimes with greenish tints. The grain varies from straight in well-grown trees, to wavy or curly, and the texture is fine, giving a smooth surface under sharp tools. The wood is hard, stiff, but inclined to be brittle, and weighs about 768 kg/m³ on average when dried.

Drying
Rather difficult to dry and requires care since it is liable to develop large, deep, and irregular checks. It is not liable to serious warping.

Strength
No information.

Durability
Very durable.

Working qualities
Although hard and dense, the wood is said to work and machine with moderate ease, and to be capable of a very smooth surface in planing and moulding.

Uses
Piling, posts, bridges, wharves, particularly where *Teredo* is a hazard, sills, doors, windows, stairs, (treads, risers, balusters, and hand-rails), siding, sheathing, framing of hemp presses and sugar mills, cog-wheels, agricultural implements, and carving and sculpture of sacred images.

NARRA

Pterocarpus indicus Willd.   Family : Leguminosae

Distribution
This species is widely distributed throughout southern and south east Asia, producing Solomons padauk and Papua New Guinea rosewood. It is found throughout the Philippines, and is abundant in Cagayan, Mindoro, Palawan and Cotabato.

The tree
A large tree with an irregular fluted trunk, attaining a height of 40m and a diameter up to 2m above the broad, flat buttress which extends some 10m to 12m up the trunk.

The timber
The sapwood is 40mm to 60mm wide, light-coloured and distinct from the heartwood which may be light yellow or brick-red in colour. Red narra is generally associated with slow-growing, and ill-formed trees, and it is said that timber from trees in Cagayan is generally harder and heavier than that from other provinces, and is blood-red in colour. The wood is often prominently figured, due to a combination of storied elements, terminal parenchyma, and grain irregularities giving rise to mottle, fiddle-back, ripple and curl effects.
The well-known name amboyna, is restricted to the highly-decorative wood produced from burrs.
The grain is interlocked, wavy, or crossed, and the texture is moderately fine. The wood varies in weight, and generally speaking the darker the wood the heavier the weight, but on average it is about 660 kg/m^3 when dried.

Drying
The timber dries rather slowly, but reasonably well, the red-coloured wood requiring more care than the yellow variety.

Strength
Strength is not a general requirement in the normal uses to which narra is put, but straight-grained material is only slightly inferior in general strength properties to European beech.

Durability
Very durable.

Working qualities
Fairly easy to work and machine, with only a slight dulling effect on cutting edges. A good finish is obtained when planing or moulding straight-grained material, but otherwise, the cutting angle should be reduced to 20° in order to obtain the best results. The timber can be nailed, screwed, and glued satisfactorily, and takes an excellent polish.

Uses
Furniture, high-class joinery, panelling, interior trim for houses and boats, decorative veneer, and as cases for scientific instruments.

OAK, JAPANESE

Quercus spp. principally   Family: Fagaceae
Q. mongolica var. *grosseserrata*

Other names
ohnara is the Japanese name for *Q. mongolica* Turcz. var. *grosseserrata* Bl. the timber of which is normally exported to Europe. Other species are usually referred to as follows, konara (*Q. glandulifera*); kashiwa (*Q. dentata*); shira-kashi (*Q. myrsinaefolia*); ichii-gashi (*Q. gilva*); aka-gashi (*Q. acuta*); ubame-gashi (*Q. phillyraeoides*).

Distribution
Ohnara, or Japanese oak, generally comes from the north island of Hokkaido, but it also occurs in the central district of the main island.

The timber
The timber is a uniform yellowish-brown, a little paler in colour than that of European or American white oak, and much milder in character, due to the slow, even growth. It weighs about 670 kg/m³ when dried. Timber from trees grown in the main island generally has a pinkish shade.

Durability
Moderately durable.

Uses
Furniture, cabinets, joinery, panelling.

PALAQUIUM SPECIES

The Sapotaceae family includes some twenty-five species of the genus *Palaquium*, of which one or more occur in practically every island and province in the Philippines.

The trees are medium-sized to large, with tall, straight trunks, and diameters up to 1.5m.

Although not as abundant as the lauans, the logs are invariably present in Manila yards, the timber sometimes being mixed with lauans and other miscellaneous red woods for local markets.

The wood of all species, except for some differences in colour, weight, and hardness, is practically identical, and local names in various regions are applied to all species almost indifferently.

The following are some of the principal species, along with their local names.

P. ahernianum Merr.	kalipaya.
P. cuneatum Vid.	malikmik.
P. foxworthyi Merr.	tagatoi.
P. gigantifolium Merr.	alakaak.
P. luzoniensis Vid.	nato.
P. merrillii Dubard.	dulitan.
P. philippense C. B. Rob..	malacmalac.
P. tenuipetiolatum Merr.	manicnic.

The timber is favoured among Filipino and Chinese cabinet-makers for furniture, particularly for drawer sides and backs, shelves, etc. because of its ease of working and freedom from warping, and timber for this type of use is generally called amugis corriente, which roughly means, normal, or usual amugis, which firstly, identifies selected wood, not necessarily of one species, and secondly, serves to distinguish it from amugis perfecto, or true amugis, which name is more properly applied to the timber of *Koordersiodendron pinnatum* Merr. a member of the Anacardiaceae family, similar in appearance to *Palaquium* species.

The various species of *Palaquium* vary from soft to moderately hard and light to moderately heavy, the wood weighing from 640 kg/m³ to 720 kg/m³ when dried. The sapwood is 20mm to 50mm wide, and in large trees sharply marked off from the heartwood which varies from light red to dull reddish-brown. The grain is straight or slightly interlocked, sometimes with a regular wave forming a diagonal ribbon figure on quarter-sawn surfaces. The texture is fine, and promotes a smooth, almost glossy finish when the wood is planed.

The timber dries easily and well, and is easy to work.

Uses
Said to be non-durable when used in contact with the ground, all the species are used for general utility purposes, often as an alternative to lauan, and is often favoured, because, despite its low resistance to decay, it is said to be rarely attacked by beetles. A good joinery, and general purpose timber for interior use.

PALDAO

Dracontomelum dao Merr. & Rolfe.   Family : Anacardiaceae

Other names
dao (Philippines).

Distribution
Various species of *Dracontomelum* occur in Papua New Guinea and neighbouring islands, producing the timber, known as Papua New Guinea walnut, but the principal species found in the Philippines is *D. dao* the source of commercial paldao or dao.

The tree
A tall, straight tree with a diameter of about 0.6m to 1.0m. In open situations the bole is often crooked, but under forest conditions this is usually straight, but always with very long, thin buttresses extending some 6m or 8m up the trunk.

The timber
The sapwood is very large, light pinkish or brownish in colour, rather sharply distinguished from the heartwood which is brownish or greenish-grey, with irregular dark brown or almost black streaks. The grain may be straight or interlocked and sometimes wavy, and a broken ribbon-grain figure often occurs on quarter-sawn faces. The texture is medium and even. The wood weighs about 740 kg/m^3 when dried.

Drying
Dries well with care, but there is a tendency for the wood to warp badly.

Strength
No information.

Durability
Moderately durable.

Working qualities
Works and machines readily, with only a moderate blunting effect on cutting edges. Interlocked grain tends to pick up in planing and moulding and a reduction of cutting angle to 20° is beneficial. The wood takes an excellent polish.

Uses
Carpentry and joinery, flooring, furniture and cabinets, etc. Locally, the buttress timber is used for decorative table tops. Good decorative veneer is produced from selected logs.

PALOSAPIS

Anisoptera thurifera Bl.   Family: Dipterocarpaceae

Distribution
Various species of *Anisoptera* produce mersawa of Malaysia, krabak of Thailand, and palosapis of the Philippines, where the principal species, *A. thurifera* occurs in primary forests, in heavy stands in most of the islands.

The tree
A large tree, reaching a height of 40m to 45m and a diameter of 1.2m to 1.8m with a straight, unbuttressed regular bole 20m to 30m in length.

The timber
The light-coloured sapwood is 50mm to 80mm wide, not very distinct from the heartwood which is buff coloured initially, turning yellowish or yellow after drying. The grain is straight, sometimes crossed or wavy, with a slight ribbon figure on quarter-sawn surfaces, and the texture is moderately fine to coarse. The wood weighs about 720 kg/m³ when dried.

Drying
Dries slowly, with a reluctance to give up its moisture from the centre of thick material. Thin sizes are susceptible to warping, and care must be taken to ensure good sticking practice. Shrinkage, green to 12 per cent moisture content is 6 per cent tangentially, and 2 per cent radially.

Strength
By comparison with tangile, the timber is about 20 per cent stiffer, slightly stronger in compression parallel to the grain, and about 40 per cent more tough.

Durability
Moderately durable.

Working qualities
Machines readily, but with a severe blunting effect on cutting edges. The rather fibrous finish obtained in planing and moulding can be improved by a reduction of cutting angle to 20°. The wood can be peeled satisfactorily for veneer.

Uses
Boat planking, plywood, interior finish, general construction, vehicle bodies.

SOPHORA

Sophora japonica L.   Family: Leguminosae

Other names
pagoda tree (UK); yen-ju, en-ju (Japan).

Distribution
S. japonica occurs in China and Japan, and a further species, *S. tetraptera*, is found in New Zealand. *S. japonica* was introduced into Britain in 1753 as an ornamental tree, its long, pinnate leaves, and graceful, bushy crown, together with its cylindrical seed pods, constricted between the seeds like a string of beads, presenting a very pleasing appearance.

General characteristics

Sophora is closely related to *Laburnum*, *Wistaria*, and *Acacia*, and the wood is of a golden-brown colour with a greenish tint, and somewhat resembling laburnum wood. It possesses a lustrous sheen, and fairly fine texture, and weighs about 673 kg/m³ when dried.

Uses

Under open growth conditions, the form of the tree generally precludes long, wide, boards, and it is unlikely that sophora will be seen on world timber markets. It is however, considered a valuable material in Japan where the strong, tough timber is used largely for pillars and house framing. It is said to be durable.

TINDALO

Pahudia rhomboidea Prain.   Family: Leguminosae

Distribution

Fairly widely distributed throughout the Philippines, but not as abundant as narra.

General characteristics

A straight, but not tall tree, with a diameter of 1.2m. The wood is hard and heavy, weighing from 772 kg/m³ to 805 kg/m³ when dried. The sapwood is whitish, 20mm to 40mm wide, and sharply distinguished from the heartwood which is saffron coloured, or pale orange, turning to a deep, rich red colour with age, sometimes with irregular blackish streaks, and occasionally with scattered bird's-eye knots. The wood has a slight odour when freshly sawn, reminiscent of peanuts.

The grain is usually straight but may be shallowly interlocked, and the texture is fine. The wood is said to dry easily and well, with only a slight tendency to warping and checking, and is fairly easy to machine, the dense, compact nature of the wood producing a smooth, almost glossy finish in planing and moulding when cutters are maintained in sharp condition.

It is moderately durable, and is considered one of the finest Philippine cabinet woods.

Uses

Interior finish, flooring, doors, windows, sills, stair treads, hand rails on account of its good colour and smooth hardness, musical instruments, cabinet making, and for all kinds of high-grade construction except posts set in the ground.

WILLOW

Salix spp.   Family: Salicaceae

Various species of willow occur throughout Europe, North Africa, Asia, etc including China and Japan, and generally provide basket-making and rough weaving material and timber. The principal Japanese species is *Salix jessoensis* Seem.

General characteristics

The Japanese name for this wood is tokachiyanigi. The sapwood is white to straw-coloured, gradually merging into the pinkish-yellow heartwood. The grain varies considerably according to the growth habit of the tree, ranging from straight to wavy, but with a fine, even texture. The wood is light in weight, about 433 kg/m^3 when dried.

Uses

Local uses include artificial limbs, clog soles, toys, lorry bottoms and for fibre board.

PART II SOFTWOODS

ALMACIGA

Agathis philippinensis Warb.   Family: Araucariaceae

Distribution
Although widely distributed throughout the Philippines, almaciga occurs rather sparsely in the higher altitudes above the Dipterocarp forests, and occasionally at sea level in a few places.

The tree
A large, tall tree, reaching a height of 60m and a diameter of 3m on good sites. The bole is straight and cylindrical, and clear of branches for 20m to 30m.

The timber
The wood is similar to kauri, being pinkish-buff in colour, with no distinction between sapwood and heartwood. The grain is straight, and the texture very fine, and the wood has neither odour nor taste. The weight is variable, depending on growth conditions and may be fairly light, or comparatively heavy, but on average it weighs about 550 kg/m³ when dried.

Drying
Dries readily and without undue degrade.

Strength
By comparison with lauan, the timber is similar to almon in general strength properties, and compared with pitch pine, it has about the same strength, except in bending strength and stiffness, where it is rather inferior.

Durability
Perishable.

Working qualities
The wood works easily and well. It has good nailing and screwing properties, and stains and polishes excellently. It has fairly

good peeling properties, and produces a high proportion of face quality veneer.

Uses
Owing to the valuable resin (Manila copal) produced by the tree, and used in the manufacture of high-grade, glossy varnishes and lacquers, the felling of almaciga is discouraged by the Philippine government in order to protect the copal industry, but almaciga wood is suitable for artificial limb manufacture, instrument cases, pencil slats, joinery and veneer.

BENGUET PINE

Pinus insularis Endl.   Family : Pinaceae

Other names
saleng, bel-bel, parina, salit.

Distribution
Occurs in a long narrow belt in the mountain area of north-west Luzon in abundant quantities, and sparsely near the coast of Zambales.

The tree
A moderately tall tree with a diameter of about 1.4m.

The timber
A hard pine of the pitch pine type. The wood is moderately hard to hard, and the heartwood is very much heavier than the sapwood, in fact in some specimens the heartwood is heavier than water. The heartwood is very resinous, ranging from pale yellow to rich orange-brown, and that from over-mature trees sometimes being almost completely impregnated with resin. There is a marked contrast between the lighter-coloured early-wood and the much darker zones of late-wood in each growth ring. The grain is generally straight, and the texture fine. The wood weighs from 673 kg/m^3 to 880 kg/m^3 or more depending on the resin content.

Drying
The timber is said to dry slowly but well.

Strength
No information.

Durability
Sapwood non-durable, heartwood durable in respect of decay, very durable in respect of insects. It is rarely if ever attacked by insects, even termites avoiding the heart and resinous knots.

Working qualities
Fairly easy to work and machine, but extreme gumminess slows most machine operations.

Uses
Used in the mountain districts for practically every utilitarian purpose. It seldom reaches the Manila market.

A further species, *Pinus merkusii* Jungh & de Vr. occurs in the interior of Mindoro and Zambales. Known as Mindoro pine, or tapulau, it is similar to benguet pine, and often even more resinous.

FIR, JAPANESE

Abies mariesii Mast.   Family: Pinaceae

Other names
todo matsu (Japan).

General characteristics
This species belongs to the same group that produces amabilis fir of North America. The wood is a little darker in colour than most species of *Abies*, due to the darker late-wood bands, and a little coarser in texture than spruce. It weighs about 416 kg/m^3 when dried.

Uses
Used separately or mixed with spruce for general utility purposes.

HEMLOCK

Tsuga spp.   Family: Pinaceae

A few species of the genus *Tsuga* occur in China and Japan, *T. chinensis* and *T. yunnanensis* growing in China, and *T.*

diversifolia and *T. sieboldii* in Japan. All these yield timber for local use, and it is doubtful if any will generally be exported.

General characteristics
The well-known western and eastern hemlock of North America belong to a group of species of *Tsuga* in which the leaves are minutely toothed, whereas the Chinese and Japanese species have entire leaves, but apart from this the timber is to all intents and purposes the same in general appearance in both groups, being non-resinous, and pale brown in colour with the darker late-wood bands having a reddish or purplish cast.

Probably the most important species is *T. sieboldii* Carr. of Japan, which weighs about 465 kg/m³ when dried, has a straight to crossed grain and a fairly coarse texture, and lacks the lustre typical in western hemlock.

Uses
General construction, carpentry and joinery, and to a minor extent for veneer.

LARCH, JAPANESE

L. kaempferi Sarg. syn.   Family: Pinaceae
L. leptolepis Gord.

Distribution
Japan, principally in Shinano Province.

The tree
Attains a height of 18m to 30m and a diameter of 0.75m.

The timber
The sapwood is light-brown in colour, sharply defined from the reddish-brown heartwood. The growth rings are clearly marked, with well-defined latewood bands. The wood is resinous, with a straight grain, and medium fine texture. It weighs about 560 kg/m³ when dried.

Drying
Dries fairly rapidly with some tendency to warp, split and check.

Strength
Although about 30 per cent softer than European larch, the timber is practically as strong.

Durability
Moderately durable.

Working qualities
The timber works readily, but since the soft, earlywood tends to crumble when planed, sharp cutting edges are needed to ensure a good finish. Knots are hard, and can be troublesome in the lower commercial grades. The wood can be painted or varnished without difficulty, but it tends to split when nailed.

Uses
General construction, furniture, flooring, bridge construction and boat building.

RED PINE, JAPANESE

Pinus densiflora   Family: Pinaceae

Other names
akamatsu

Distribution
Widely distributed from Kyushu to Hokkaido in Japan.

General characteristics
The sapwood is whitish in colour, and the heartwood is light reddish-brown, of the soft pine type, similar in strength properties to European redwood, with a straight grain, and fine texture, weighing about 400 kg/m³. Non-durable, it is used locally for building construction, joinery, panelling and boat building. The timber is inclined to be knotty, and is difficult to obtain in relatively clear stock.

SPRUCE, JAPANESE

Picea jezoensis Carr.   Family: Pinaceae
syn. *P. ajanensis* Fisch.

Other names
yeddo spruce (UK) ; yezo matsu (Japan).

General characteristics

The spruces can be divided into two basic groups, ie those in which the leaves are flattened or distinctly 2-edged, with grey lines on one side only, and those with quadrangular section leaves with grey line on both sides. Norway and Canadian spruce belong to this latter group, while Sitka spruce, and yeddo spruce belong to the former, accordingly, Japanese, or yeddo spruce has more of the characteristics of Sitka spruce, than of European spruce or whitewood.

The timber is non-resinous, without odour, and non-tainting, whitish in colour, often with a pinkish cast, mainly straight-grained, but sometimes with spiral grain, and weighing about 432 kg/m³ when dried.

Uses

The timber is non-durable, and is used locally for utilitarian purposes in building and joinery, and is often mixed with fir.

SUGI

Cryptomeria japonica D. Don.   Family: Taxodiaceae

Other name

Japanese cedar.

Distribution

Japan and Taiwan.

The tree

Under favourable conditions the tree attains a height of 45m or more, and a diameter of 2m and occasionally much more.

The timber

Sugi is related to sequoia and swamp cypress, and in appearance is similar to the latter, being a warm brown colour with yellow or dark brown streaks forming a somewhat wavy pattern, but it is harder, and firmer textured than cypress.

A feature of sugi is the resin which occurs mainly in vertical parenchyma cells, and is black in colour. This tends to glisten on longitudinal surfaces, and imparts a slight lustre to the wood, which is straight-grained, and weighs about 400 kg/m³ when dried.

Drying
Requires care, particularly in thick sizes, since there is a definite tendency for the wood to split and check.

Strength
No information.

Durability
Durable.

Working qualities
Saws and machines with only a moderate blunting effect on cutting edges, due mainly to the resin, but knots can be troublesome in planing and moulding since the tendency for the grain to tear is increased in the vicinity of knots. With care, the wood can be finished smoothly, and it takes the usual finishing treatments quite well. It tends to split in nailing, but holds screws well.

Uses
For centuries, the tree has been venerated by the Japanese, the mysticism and pious sentiment being restricted to the growing tree, not the timber, which has rarely been cultivated, with the result that this is usually rather knotty, although the tree is capable of producing much clear timber. It is used for house framing, gate-ways to temples, and for joinery and furniture frames.

USE GUIDE FOR PHILIPPINE AND JAPANESE TIMBERS

AGRICULTURAL IMPLEMENTS

agoho
almaciga
aranga
Diospyros spp. (sapwood)
guijo
larch
malabayabas

mangachapuy
mengkulang
merbau
molave
pine, benguet
yacal

BEARINGS, BUSHINGS, COGS AND PULLEYS

boxwood   malabayabas   mancono

BOAT AND SHIP CONSTRUCTION

Decking
apitong
guijo
larch
lauan, red

mangachapuy
mengkulang
palosapis
yacal

Framing
mengkulang

molave

Keels and stems
aranga
guijo
liusin

molave
yacal

Masts and spars
guijo (small spars)
lauan, red (small spars)

malagai
mangachapuy

Oars and paddles
almaciga (light sculls and paddles)
calantas   lauan, white   molave

Planking
guijo
larch
lauan, red
lauan, white

mangachapuy
mengkulang
palosapis
yacal

Superstructures
banuyo
calantas
lauan, red
mengkulang

narra
oak
Palaquium spp.
tindalo

BOXES AND CRATES

Cigar boxes
calantas (high-grade)

lauan, light red (cheap-grade)

Clothes chests

narra

chestnut, horse

hemlock

Packing cases
apitong
fir
guijo
hemlock
mengkulang

palosapis
pine, benguet
pine, red
spruce

Scientific instrument cases
lauan, red

narra.

CONSTRUCTION

Heavy
agoho
amugis
aranga
binggas

malabayabas
merbau
molave

Light
acle
agaru
almaciga

apitong
batete
beech

Light *(continued)*

birch
calamansanay
calantas
fir
hemlock
keyaki
larch

oak
Palaquium spp.
palosapis
pine, benguet
pine, red
spruce
suqi

DOORS

agaru
apitong
ash
banuyo
batete
baticulin, yellow
guijo
hemlock
lauan, red
mangachapuy

mengkulang
merbau
molave
narra
oak
Palaquium spp.
palosapis
tangile
tindalo

FANCY GOODS AND NOVELTIES

agaru
alder (gnarled pieces)
aranga
birch
bolong-eta (sapwood stained
    black)
boxwood
calamansanay
camagon (sapwood stained black)

cherry
Diospyros spp.
kaki
kiri
malabayabas
mancono
molave
narra
tindalo

FLOORING

agaru
amugis
apitong
aranga
ash

batete
beech
binggas
calamansanay
fir

66

FLOORING *(continued)*

guijo
hemlock
larch
malagai
mangachapuy
maple
mengkulang
merbau
molave

narra
oak
Palaquium spp.
paldao
palosapis
tangile
tindalo
yacal

FURNITURE AND CABINETS

agaru
ash
batete
banuyo
baticulin, yellow
beech
calantas
cherry
Diospyros spp.
guijo
kaki

katsura
kiri
lauan
maple
mengkulang
merbau
narra
oak
paldao
tangile
tindalo

JOINERY

High-class
acle
agaru
ash
banuyo
calantas
cherry
katsura
keyaki

larch
lauan, red
maple
narra
oak
paldao
tindalo

Utility
almaciga
amugis
aranga

banuyo
batete
baticulin, yellow

JOINERY Utility *(continued)*

beech
birch
calamansanay
fir
hemlock
lanipau
larch

Palaquium spp.
palosapis
pine, benguet
pine, red
spruce
sugi

MARINE PILING AND CONSTRUCTION

Under water
a Teredo infested waters
agoho
liusin

mancono
molave

b Non-Teredo waters
in addition to above,
agaru
aranga

calamansanay
merbau
yacal

Above water
a Docks, wharves, bridges, etc.
agoho
aranga
apitong
binggas
calamansanay
larch

mengkulang
merbau
malabayabas
mangachapuy
palosapis
yacal

b Decking
aranga
apitong

calamansanay
yacal

MUSICAL INSTRUMENTS

apitong (harp bases)
banuyo
baticulin, yellow
bolong-eta
calamansanay

calantas
camagon
ebony
kiri
lauan

MUSICAL INSTRUMENTS *(continued)*

malatinta	palosapis
merbau	tangile
narra	tindalo
paldao	tiaong

SCULPTURE AND CARVING

a Sacred images and statues

baticulin, yellow	merbau
calantas	molave
lauan, red	tangile

b Andas (litter or bier on which saints or statues are carried)

acle	lauan (low cost)
banuyo	narra

c Permanent pedestals and platforms for images and statues
molave

d Altars and ornamental fixtures in churches

acle	tindalo
narra	

e Carved feet, panels and finials for furniture

acle	keyaki
baticulin, yellow	molave
calantas	narra
Diospyros spp.	tangile
katsura	tindalo

SPORTS GOODS

agaru	calamansanay
agoho	calantas
almaciga	camagon (sapwood)
aranga	camagon (heartwood)
ash	guijo
ata-ata (sapwood)	kaki
bolong-eta (sapwood)	lauan

SPORTS GOODS *(continued)*

malabayabas
mangachapuy
mancono
maple
mengkulang

merbau
molave
narra
tindalo
yacal

STAIRS

a Balusters and handrails

apitong
aranga
batete
calamansanay
guijo
lauan
mangachapuy
maple

mengkulang
merbau
molave
narra
oak
Palaquium spp.
tindalo

b Treads and risers

maple
molave

tindalo

generally preferred, but any of **a** also used.

TURNERY

alder
beech
birch
boxwood
cherry

kaki
mancono
maple
oak
tindalo

VEHICLE BODIES

amugis
apitong
guijo
lauan
mangachapuy

merbau
narra
palosapis
willow (bottoms)
yacal

VENEER AND PLYWOOD

a Corestock

fir
hemlock

lauan, white
spruce

Decorative

agaru
ash
batete
birch
bolong-eta
camagon
ebony
keyaki

malatinta
maple
molave
narra (amboyna)
oak
paldao (selected)
tindalo

c Utility (plywood, chip-baskets, small laminted items, etc)

alder
almaciga
ash
beech
birch
hemlock

kiri
lauan
malagai
palosapis
spruce

TERMITE RESISTANCE

Termite activity represents a serious hazard to timber structures in the Philippines, particularly to house foundations. The use of timbers which offer some natural resistance to termite attack minimises the generally disastrous effect of termites, but chemical soil treatments at the time of building, and preservative and insecticidal pressure treatment of building timber, not only widens the range of suitable timbers, but offers greater protection to termite attack.

Physical barrier systems, such as termite caps, incorporated into the construction of buildings must be free from perforation and form a continuous barrier, but they cannot entirely be relied upon to offer suitable safeguards against termite attack.

The following list of timbers is grouped according to their natural resistance to termite attack, and is based primarily on local preferences and traditional use, and not necessarily on the results of field tests. The classification is based on the resistance of heartwood, unless otherwise stated.

Very resistant

acle	mancono
calantas	merbau
liusin	molave
malabayabas	narra

Resistant

agaru	*Diospyros* spp. heartwood
agoho	mengkulang
aranga	*Palaquium* spp.
binggas	

Moderately resistant

amugis	kaki
apitong	mangachapuy
banuyo	paldao
calamansanay	tindalo
Diospyros spp. (sapwood)	yacal

Very susceptible

alder	katsura
almaciga	larch
ash	malagai
batete	maple
beech	palosapis
birch	pine, benguet
cherry	pine, red
chestnut, horse	spruce
fir	sugi
hemlock	willow

AMENABILITY OF HEARTWOOD TO PRESERVATIVE TREATMENT

Extremely resistant

agoho	liusin
Albizia spp.	malabayabas
amugis	malagai
aranga	mancono
Diospysos spp.	merbau
Hopea spp.	molave
kaki	*Palaquium* spp.
guijo	

Resistant

agaru	larch
almaciga	lauan
banuyo	narra
batete	oak
baticulin	paldao
fir	spruce
hemlock	tindalo
katsura	

Moderately resistant

ailanthus	calantas
ash	keyaki
binggas	lumbayao
calamansanay	

Permeable

alder
beech
birch
chestnut, horse

maple
pine, red
willow

AMENABILITY OF HEARTWOOD TO PRESERVATIVE TREATMENT

The above classification refers to the ease with which a timber absorbs preservatives under both open-tank (non-pressure) and pressure treatments. Sapwood, although nearly always perishable, is usually much more permeable than heartwood, accordingly, the above classification refers to the relative resistance of heartwood to penetration.

Extremely resistant
Timbers that absorb only a small amount of preservative even under long pressure treatments. They cannot be penetrated to an appreciable depth laterally, and only to a very small extent longitudinally.

Resistant
Timbers difficult to impregnate under pressure and require a long period of treatment. It is often difficult to penetrate them laterally more than about 3mm to 6mm.
Incising is often used to obtain better treatment.

Moderately resistant
Timbers that are fairly easy to treat, and it is usually possible to obtain a lateral penetration of the order of 6mm to 18mm in about 2-3 hours under pressure, or a penetration of a large proportion of the vessels.

Permeable
Timbers that can be penetrated completely under pressure without difficulty, and can usually be heavily impregnated by the open-tank process.

REFERENCES

BRITISH STANDARDS INSTITUTION. Nomenclature of commercial timbers, including sources of supply. British Standard BS 881 & 589. London, BSI. 1974.

BUILDING RESEARCH ESTABLISHMENT. Handbook of hardwoods, revised by R. H. Farmer. London, HMSO. 1972.

BUILDING RESEARCH ESTABLISHMENT. A handbook of softwoods. BRE Report. London, HMSO. 2nd ed. 1977.

PHILIPPINES. FOREST PRODUCTS RESEARCH AND INDUSTRIES DEVELOPMENT COMMISSION. Philippine Timber Series Nos. 1-14. Laguna, FPRIDC. nd.

HOWARD, Alexander L. A manual of timbers of the world. London, Macmillan & Co. Ltd. 3rd ed. 1948.

JANE, F. W. The structure of wood, revised by K. Wilson and D. J. B. White. London, Adam & Charles Black. 2nd ed. 1970.

ANON. Philippine timbers. 1946.

The TRADA series of red booklets—'Timbers of the World'

1 Timbers of Africa

2 Timbers of South America

3 Timbers of Southern Asia

4 Timbers of South East Asia

5 Timbers of Philippines and Japan

6 Timbers of Europe

7 Timbers of North America

8 Timbers of Australasia

9 Timbers of Central America and Caribbean

INDEX

81